Discovering Cultures

Nigeria

Patricia J. Murphy

BENCHMARK BOOKS

MARSHALL CAVENDISH
NEW YORK

For my nephew, Erik, with love—*P.J.M.*

Marshall Cavendish
99 White Plains Road
Tarrytown, New York 10591-9001
www.marshallcavendish.com

Text copyright © 2005 by Marshall Cavendish Corporation
Map and illustrations copyright © 2005 by Marshall Cavendish Corporation

All Internet sites were available and accurate when sent to press.

Library of Congress Cataloging-in-Publication Data

Murphy, Patricia J., 1963–
Nigeria / by Patricia J. Murphy.
p. cm. — (Discovering cultures)
Includes bibliographical references and index.
ISBN 0-7614-1795-8
1. Nigeria—Juvenile literature. I. Title. II. Series.
DT515.22.M87 2005
966.9—dc22   2004006129

Photo Research by Candlepants Incorporated
Cover Photo: Friedrich Stark/Das Fotoarchiv/*Peter Arnold, Inc.*

The photographs in this book are used by permission and through the courtesy of; *Peter Arnold Inc.*: Larissa Siebicke/Das Fotoarchiv, 1; Martin Harvey, 4; Mark Edwards/Still Pictures, 9, 42 (right); Andreas Buck/Das Fotoarchiv, 14-15, 20-21, 36, 43 (lower right); I.Uwanaka/UNEP, 32 (right). *Photo Researchers Inc*: Georg Gerster, 6; Peter Bowater, 43 (lower left). *Corbis*: Paul Almasy, 7, 11, 12 (right), 18, 19, 30, 43 (top left); North Carolina Museum of Art, 16; James Marshall, 22, 23, 26, 27; Liba Taylor, 28; Reuters, 31, 32 (left), 45; Brooks Craft, 44; Kerstin Geier, back cover. *PANOS Pictures*: Betty Press, 10, 12 (left); Giles Moberly, 39. *Werner Forman/Art Resource, NY*: 13. *Steven Needham/Envision*: 24. *The Image Works*: Carol Beckwith & Angela Fisher/HAGA, 34-35, 37, 38.

Cover: *The main mosque in Abuja*; Title page: *A Hausa girl*

Map and illustrations by Ian Warpole
Book design by Virginia Pope

Printed in China
1 3 5 6 4 2

Turn the Pages...

Where in the World Is Nigeria?

Nigeria is a country of different lands, warm temperatures, and even warmer people. Called the Federal Republic of Nigeria, it is found on the west coast of Africa. This country stretches over 356,670 square miles (923,770 square kilometers). It is nearly two times the size of California. Nigeria borders several countries and the Atlantic Ocean. To the north is Niger; to the East are Chad and Cameroon. West of Nigeria is Benin. In the South, there are 500 miles of coast on the Gulf of Guinea. Its waters flow into the Atlantic Ocean.

The Nigerian countryside

Map of Nigeria

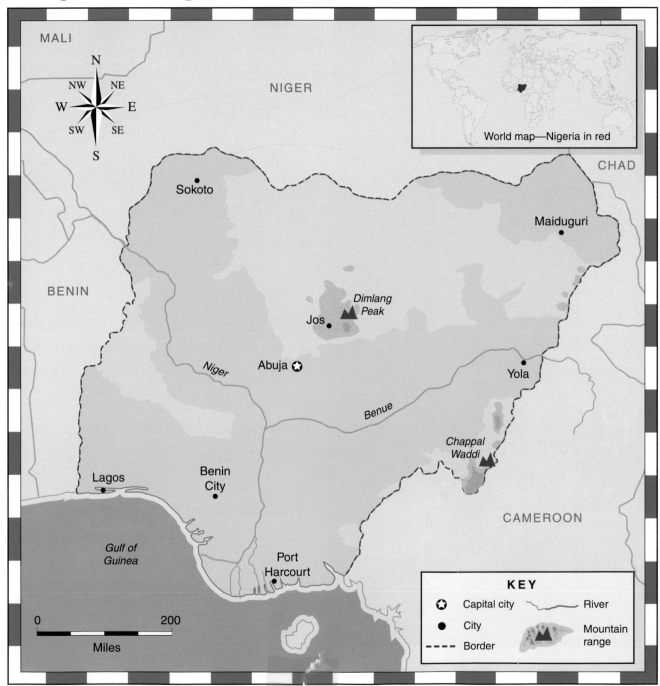

MALI

N
NW · NE
W · E
SW · SE
S

NIGER

World map—Nigeria in red

CHAD

Sokoto

Maiduguri

BENIN

Dimlang
Peak

Jos

Niger

Abuja ✪

Yola

Benue

Chappal
Waddi

Benin
City

CAMEROON

Lagos

Gulf of
Guinea

Port
Harcourt

0   200

Miles

KEY

✪ Capital city   River

● City   Mountain
                       range

- - - Border

The country of Nigeria is divided into thirty-six states and one capital territory. The capital of Nigeria is the city of Abuja. It is right in the center of the country. Nigeria's largest city is Lagos. Until 1991, it was the capital of Nigeria. Nigerians chose Abuja as their new capital because Lagos became too crowded and was far away from everything. Now, Lagos is Nigeria's business center. Television and radio shows are also produced there.

The busy city of Lagos, Nigeria

Different landforms make up Nigeria. Beginning in the west, Nigeria's sandy beaches turn into regions of mangrove swamps. Mangroves are *tropical* shrubs and trees with huge roots that stand up out of the water. The swamps are filled with salty water and shaded by many trees.

Moving closer to the center of Nigeria, the land becomes wetter and the air becomes humid. A wonderland of old walnut and mahogany trees and wildlife fill the rain forest. From the forest floor to treetops, African gorillas, monkeys, wildcats, crocodiles, snakes, and birds build their homes.

Nigeria's center is covered with plateaus of rolling grasses and woodlands. Plateaus are high, flat lands. Dimlang Peak on the Jos Plateau reaches 6,690 feet (2,040 meters). The country's highest point is in the east at Chappal Waddi. This mountain is 7,937 feet (2,419 m) tall. North of the plateaus is Nigeria's hottest and driest land, the semidesert. A semidesert is an area between a desert and a grassland or woodland. It usually gets only 10 to 20 inches (25 to 51 centimeters) of rain a year.

In the southwest, the Niger River empties into the Gulf of Guinea and into the Atlantic Ocean. Together, Nigeria's two main rivers—the Niger in the south, and the Benue in the west, split Nigeria into three parts. The rivers act as natural borders that separate three of Nigeria's largest *ethnic* groups—the Hausa, the Yoruba, and the Igbo. Other rivers, lakes, creeks, and lagoons zigzag the land.

A view of Kano, Nigeria

Because Nigeria is just above the equator, most of the country has a tropical climate. Nigeria has two main seasons—the rainy season, which lasts from April to October, and the dry season, which is from November to March. Sometimes, it rains so much that it floods. Fifty inches (127 cm) of rain fall in central Nigeria each year and up to 170 inches (432 cm) fall in the south. At other times, there are droughts. The southwest and harmattan winds play a part in Nigeria's weather. The harmattan blows hot, dry wind from the northwest. It carries a desert dust that colors everything red. In the north, the harmattan brings cold temperatures and a strong wind from the Sahel desert. The wind blows sand from the desert that covers the northern cities. Sometimes, when the wind is blowing, people cannot see anything.

Nigeria's rich land and tropical climate make it easy to grow its main crops such as cotton and peanuts. Below the ground, many resources such as natural gas and crude oil are collected. Nigeria is one of the world's largest producers of oil.

Unfortunately, farming and oil have not made much money for Nigeria. The country must find better ways to manage its resources to provide more money for its people.

A natural gas platform off the Nigerian coast

The Niger River

Nigeria's largest river, the Niger, is Africa's third-largest. It is also the river
that gave Nigeria its name. The Niger has been both kind and cruel to Nigeria.
For many years, it has allowed Nigerians to ship goods and to travel from place
to place. It has supplied water for growing crops and for electrical power. But,
during the rainy season, the river floods. These floods push rich soil out of the
river and onto the land. This soil has helped farmers to grow good crops,
but it has also damaged homes and taken lives. At the mouth of
the Niger River is the Niger Delta. It has the richest soil
anywhere in Nigeria.

What Makes Nigeria Nigerian?

Nigerian children

Nigeria is home to more than 137 million people—and it is still growing. It has the most people of any African country. Nigeria's early people can be traced back 12,000 years.

In ancient times, royal empires ruled the land. Members of the royal family wore turbans instead of crowns. Royal councils decided who would rule. Later, Great Britain claimed Nigeria as one of its *colonies*. It sold many Nigerians as slaves. In 1960, Nigeria became independent from Britain. The country changed its name to the Federal Republic of Nigeria in 1963. Over the years, the country has often been under military rule.

Nigerian residents belong to one of more than 250 different ethnic groups. These groups are spread throughout Nigeria's large cities and small villages. Each

A Hausa man wears a head wrap.

of these groups has its own history, ancestors, and language. Their members practice their own customs and traditions and celebrate their own holidays. They also see and experience the world in different ways. These differences keep the ethnic groups living separate lives. They have also caused power struggles, fights over natural resources, and a civil war. Because of this, Nigeria is more like a region of separate nations than just one.

Three of the largest ethnic groups in Nigeria are the Hausa, the Yoruba, and the Igbo peoples. The Hausa are farmers and herders of cattle, sheep, and goats. They live in the northwest. Some are long-distance traders. Others are public officials or are part of the military. They follow a religion called Islam.

The Yoruba live in the southwest. Yorubas are farmers or traders. The Igbo live in southeast Nigeria. Some work for large international companies. Many Igbo are fishermen and craftsmen. Some Igbo people work in Nigeria's oil industry or in government.

Nigerians speak more than 250 different languages. While English became Nigeria's official language during British rule, it is most Nigerians' second language.

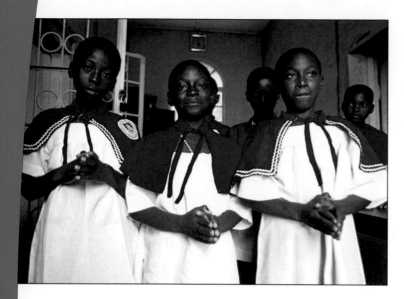

Christian altar boys

A Muslim girl reads the Quran.

To speak with other ethnic groups, Nigerians may use *pidgin* English. Pidgin English mixes English words and phrases with those from Nigeria's other ethnic languages. At school, Nigerian children learn their ethnic language along with English or French. Nigerians use English for business and governmental matters. Many Nigerian businessmen also speak French so they can do business with French-speaking countries.

While Nigerians may speak many different languages, most follow one of two religions. More than half of all Nigerians are Muslim. They practice the Islamic faith. Forty percent are Christians. The remaining 10 percent of Nigerians follow traditional African religions that worship many different gods and spirits. Some Nigerian Muslims and Christians may also have traditional African religious beliefs.

Nigeria's people have created beautiful art. The ancient Nok shaped clay into small figures with large heads. Others molded bronze sculptures and carved wooden masks. Artisans wove yarns and dyed cloth. Others crafted leather, metal, wood, and soap into prized pieces of art. Many of these artistic traditions continue today in Nigeria's *rural* villages.

Nigeria's traditional clothing is another expression of art. A person can tell the ethnic group, religion,

An ancient Nok head

and social status of the wearer by their clothes. Fabrics are woven, embroidered, and dyed. Women wear *wrappers* (wraparound skirts) and baggy shirts with headscarves, head wraps, and beaded jewelry. Men may wear long robes, baggy shirts and pants, and caps. Muslim women must cover their heads as part of their religious beliefs. In cities, Nigerians may wear clothes similar to those worn in the United States or mix traditional clothing with American-style jeans or shirts.

Lively Nigerian music provides the beat to celebrations from birth and adulthood to marriage and death. Dance mixes movements and feelings. Whether it is JuJu played with guitars, the beat of Fiji's drums, the modern mix of Afro-beat, or today's hip-hop, music is part of Nigerians' lives. Two of Nigeria's most famous musicians are King Sunny Ade and Fela Nikulapo.

A Yoruba family in front of their house

From musicians to storytellers, Nigerians have always had something to say. Early storytellers spun tales to explain the world and to teach important lessons. Nigerian writers and poets record history and the people's joys, sorrows, and hopes. They have won international awards and have fans around the world. Nigerian Wole Soyinka was the first African to win the Nobel Prize in Literature in 1986. Nigerian's booming film industry is the largest in Africa.

A Yoruba grass cloth beaded crown

Batik Design

Batik design is a technique used for dyeing clothes. Wherever wax is placed on the fabric, the dye will not appear. Ask an adult to help you try it—or dye it!

Materials:

cotton shirt

large piece of cardboard

pencil

water

candle

paintbrush

vegetable dye

newspaper

rubber gloves

long tongs

Directions:

1. Pull a T-shirt over a piece of cardboard. Draw a simple design on the front of the shirt.

2. Heat a large pot of water to a low boil.

3. Put a candle in a smaller pot. Place the smaller pot on top of the water in the large pot until the candle melts.

4. Carefully, dip your paintbrush into the wax. Using the melted wax, paint the areas where you do not want the dye to stick. Let your design dry until the wax hardens.

5. Put on rubber gloves. Using the long tongs, dip the shirt into a large tub of dye. Keep dipping your shirt until you get the color that you want.

6. Take the shirt out and rinse it in hot water. Peel off wax.

7. Hang the shirt to dry.

8. Wear it!

Living in Nigeria

Most Nigerians live in rural villages. Others live in large, modern cities. Often, their lives seem worlds apart.

Villagers farm the land or raise cattle. They grow food for their families such as beans, grains, rice, cassava, and yams. Other farmers grow cotton, peanuts, and rubber plants. These are sold to Nigerian factories and to other countries.

Along Nigeria's rivers and lakes and in the Gulf of Guinea, fishermen catch shrimp and other seafood. Miners dig for minerals and metals such as tin, columbite, coal, lead,

A man sits in front of his farmhouse.

Homes and other buildings in a Nigerian city

iron ore, zinc, limestone, and gold. They drill for natural gas and *crude oil*. Crafters make pottery, baskets, cloth, leather, carvings, jewelry, and sculpture.

While Nigeria is the world's sixth-largest producer of crude oil, few Nigerians work in this rich industry. Fewer earn any money from it. Most Nigerians make less than 350 nairas (one U.S. dollar) a week. The country is trying to find ways to develop its oil industry without the help of other countries. This will mean more jobs and money for Nigeria. Then there will be more money for new schools, doctors and hospitals, better electricity, and safer drinking water.

A Nigerian woman works in a rice factory.

Nigerian newspaper reporters at work

Nigerians may be teachers or hotel workers. Some may work for the government or in factories making paper and pulp, rubber, cement, *textiles*, soft drinks, or cigarettes. Other Nigerians own businesses or sell goods in outdoor markets.

After work, many Nigerians return to their compounds. A compound is a group of small homes where one family lives. Parents, children, grandparents, aunts, uncles, and cousins all live in the same compound. In villages, homes are made of mud, grass, and bamboo or concrete with tin roofs. Many homes do not have electricity or running water.

A busy outdoor market in Lagos

Daily life in Nigeria has its problems. Rural villagers have many health fears. They may get *malaria* from mosquitoes or get very sick from tsetse flies. Acquired immune deficiency syndrome (AIDS) is also another disease that takes the lives of Nigerians. Many Nigerians die from these diseases because they cannot afford proper medical care or because none is available in their area.

Sometimes, villagers move to the city with hopes of finding work and a better life. What they find instead are crowded cities and few jobs. Often, they also find air and water pollution, crime, drug abuse, and AIDS. Some Nigerians must move to other African countries to find work.

Each day, Nigerian families try to eat their main meal together. It may be a combination of beans, nuts, soup, porridge, rice, *akara*, fruits, vegetables, yams, cassava, and spices. Wealthy families may also have chicken or other meats. Nigerians cook with palm oil and drink palm wine. Water is often unsafe to drink.

Nigerian cooks often prepare more than their families need. If people drop by, there is enough food to share. Eating with family and friends is an important part of the Nigerian day.

Goat stew

Let's Eat!
Akara

Ingredients
1 lb. dried black-eyed peas
1 large onion, minced
Salt
Vegetable oil

Wash your hands. Ask an adult to help you.
First, soak the beans in a large bowl of water overnight. Drain the beans. Remove the skins of the beans and mash them. Add minced onion and salt. Place vegetable oil in a pan. Put oil on low heat. Wait for oil to heat up. Drop "balls" of the mixture into the pan of vegetable oil. Make sure all sides of each ball are fried until dark brown. Place on a paper towel to drain. Add salt and pepper to taste. Serve with syrup or spicy hot sauce.

School Days

Nigeria's school system has changed through the years. Long ago, missionaries taught Nigerians English so they could read the Bible. They also set up Nigeria's first schools.

Nigerian law says that children must attend school from ages six to fifteen. Today, many Nigerian children begin learning in preschool. After preschool, children enter primary school where they will stay from kindergarten to sixth grade.

Primary school in Nigeria is free. The government pays for all children to attend. In primary school, children learn math, English, religion, science, and their ethnic language. Children may attend public or private primary schools. Private schools may also offer classes in computers, French, and art. In the north, Muslim children attend religious schools. These students study the holy book called the Quran and learn about the Islamic faith.

Children wait for school to begin.

A Nigerian student takes notes.

After primary school, children can attend six years of secondary, or high school. Unfortunately, secondary school is not free in Nigeria. Because of this, fewer Nigerian children attend secondary school than primary school. Many Nigerian families do not have the money.

The first three years of secondary school are called junior secondary school. In junior secondary school, Nigerian children take classes in English, math, language, science, social studies, and religion. Junior secondary students might also participate in health, physical education, art, French, and craft classes.

To move on to senior secondary school, children must pass a special test. Once in senior secondary school, students begin to prepare for college or a job. Classes at the senior secondary school level might include English, math, science, history, geography, and literature. At the end of senior secondary school, Nigerian

At work on the computer

students must take an exam to graduate. Some students may continue their education for four years in college. Others may go to teacher colleges, technical schools, or trade schools.

Before entering the working world, college graduates must work for one year in the National Youth Service Corps. Like the U.S. Peace Corps, these workers serve their country by helping the poor.

Nigerian schools and the quality of education students receive are different from state to state. Many poor areas of Nigeria do not have the money to build schools, hire teachers, or provide supplies that wealthier areas can afford.

Nigeria's government is working to offer the best education to all children. Better-educated Nigerians will help Nigeria grow stronger. They will help the country further develop its many natural resources and industries.

Nigeria's National Pledge

Nigerian students may begin their day by reciting the country's national pledge:

I pledge to Nigeria my country
To be faithful, loyal, and honest
To serve Nigeria with all my strength
To defend her unity and uphold her honor and glory
So help me God.

Just for Fun

Whether they live in a village or in a city, Nigerians' favorite activity is to visit with family and friends. When they visit, they like to eat and tell stories. They also like to sing and dance.

Nigerian women dancing together

Nigerians like to play the number one national pastime, soccer. This sport was brought to Nigeria by the British. Soccer brings large groups of people together. Nigeria's national team, the Green Eagles, has many fans and many titles. It won the African Nations Cup in 1994 and a gold medal at the 1996 Olympic Games.

Throughout history, Nigerians have competed in wrestling, boxing, archery, cricket, and track and field. Nigerian boxers have won gold medals. Its long-distance runners have won praise. Some athletes have left the country to train and compete in the United States.

Soccer in Nigeria

Nigerians enjoy swimming and fishing along the coast of the Atlantic Ocean and in rivers and lakes. Wealthy Nigerians enjoy boating and playing polo or

Fishing in a river

A young boy drinks water from a banana leaf.

cricket. Many people go to horse races. They also play board games and table tennis, field hockey, handball, and basketball.

In cities, Nigerians go to movies, the theater, and musical concerts. Some own televisions or stereos. In villages, women visit while doing housework and fix each other's hair. Men talk while sipping palm wine. Children play with homemade toys built from clay, cornstalks, or paper.

Ayo

What do you get when you take two players, add one egg carton, two cups, and some beans, seeds, or pebbles? You get a fun game you can play for hours.

What you need:

1 egg carton

Two paper cups or "banks"

48 seeds, beans, or small pebbles
(24 for each player)

How to play:

1. Each player chooses one side of the egg carton for his territory.

2. Each player takes their 24 seeds and places four in each of their six egg carton cups.

3. To start the game, one player takes his seeds (four at first) out of one of his six egg carton cups and places one in each cup, moving clockwise.

4. If the last seed lands in one of his opponent's cups, the player can "capture" all the seeds from that cup and put them in his bank.

5. Players keep taking turns until one player either cannot move or cannot take any seeds from his cups.

6. The person with the most seeds in their bank at the end of the game wins!

Let's Celebrate!

Nigerians have many reasons and seasons to celebrate throughout the year. They observe many national and religious holidays as well as a variety of ethnic celebrations and festivals.

Nigeria's national holidays include New Year's Day on January 1, and Labor Day on May 1. They also celebrate National Day on October 1. On National Day, people remember when Nigeria became a free republic. During these holidays, Nigerians listen to speeches, attend special ceremonies, and watch parades. They also pass the time with family and friends, enjoying the day off from work or school.

Muslims and Christians in Nigeria observe important religious holidays each year. During the Muslim holiday of Ramadan, Muslims remember the blessings they have received and pray for those who are in need. For the thirty days of Ramadan, Muslims fast. They do not eat or drink from sunrise to sunset. After sunset, Muslims gather with family and friends for a large meal. Ramadan ends with the three-day festival of Eid El-Fitr. During this festival, Muslims eat special rolls and cakes and give money to the poor. They also get new clothes

Celebrating the end of Ramadan

A Christian Nativity scene

and give out food. Children dress up and go around asking for treats. In the north, some families sacrifice a goat or a sheep.

Christians celebrate Christmas and Easter. At Christmas, they celebrate the birth of Christ. To honor this day, they send Christmas cards and exchange small gifts. On Christmas Eve or Christmas Day, they go to church and gather for large family meals.

On Good Friday, Christians mourn the death of Christ. On Easter Sunday, they celebrate his rebirth. Christians observe the Easter holidays by going to church and sharing meals with family and friends. Some have picnics or go out for special dinners.

Nigeria's hundreds of ethnic groups celebrate many different festivals. Some of these festivals mark special family occasions or harvests. One of the most popular Igbo festivals is the Yam Festival. During this two-day festival, Nigerians celebrate the harvest of the yam, a type of sweet potato. People give thanks for their good yam harvest and pray for blessings for the next yam harvest.

Another Nigerian celebration is called the masquerade. Nigerians believe that the spirits of their ancestors come down and take over their bodies during this traditional religious celebration. They wear masks and dress up like the spirits.

Dressed for a harvest festival

Whatever the holiday—national, religious, or ethnic—Nigerians celebrate with food, music, and dance.

A masquerade dance

The Arungu Fishing Festival

During February and March, along the Arungu River, Nigerian fishermen celebrate the end of the harvest with the Arungu Fishing Festival.

First, drummers in canoes and men with seed-filled gourds call the fish to enter shallow waters. Fishermen wait there with their fishnets. The nets fill with hundreds of fish—from Nile perch to balloon fish. After catching the fish, Nigerians have diving contests, or go swimming, canoe racing, wild duck hunting, and bare-handed fishing. Some people gamble, while others dance and eat.

Over the years, the festival and the Arungu fishing village have grown. To house the festival's growing crowd, the people have built many hotels. The villagers hope more people will visit the Arungu Fishing Festival each year.

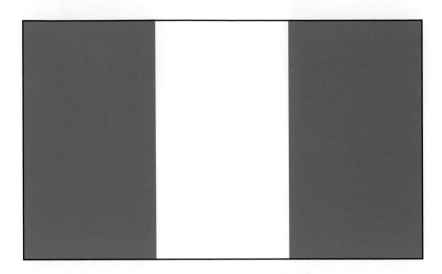

The Federal Republic of Nigeria's flag is divided into three vertical bands of green, white, and green. The green represents Nigeria's forests, farming industry, and Islam. The white represents peace and unity. Nigeria adopted the flag in 1960 when it became independent from Great Britain.

Nigeria's money is called the naira. The exchange rate often changes, but 132 nairas equaled one U.S. dollar in 2004.

Count in Hausa

English	Hausa	Say it like this:
one	daya	DI-ya
two	biyu	BEE-yoo
three	uku	ukoo
four	hudu	hoodoo
five	biyar	bee-YARR
six	shida	shi-DA
seven	bokwai	BAK-woi
eight	takwas	TAK-was
nine	tara	taaraa
ten	goma	go-MA

Glossary

akara   A Nigerian meal made with beans.

batik   A process of dyeing cloth using wax designs.

colony   A territory that is ruled by another country.

crude oil   Oil that is found in its natural or raw state in the ground.

ethnic   Related to a group of people who have the same language or culture.

malaria   A disease carried by mosquitoes that causes chills, high fevers, and sweating.

pidgin English   A type of broken English used by many Nigerians.

rural   Having to do with the countryside.

textile   A fabric that is made by weaving or knitting.

tropical   Warm and moist. A climate similar to the tropics, near the equator.

Fast Facts

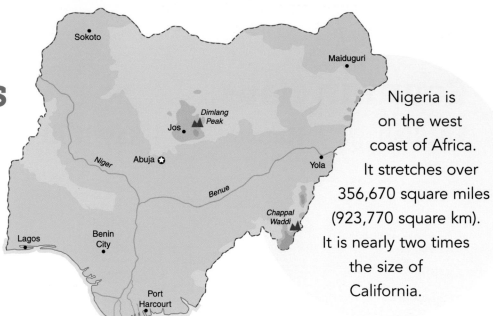

The country of Nigeria is divided into thirty-six states and one capital territory. The capital of Nigeria is the city of Abuja. It is right in the center of the country.

Nigeria is on the west coast of Africa. It stretches over 356,670 square miles (923,770 square km). It is nearly two times the size of California.

Nigeria's official name is the Federal Republic of Nigeria. The government is run by a president who is elected by the people.

Dimlang Peak on the Jos Plateau reaches 6,690 feet (2,040 m). The country's highest point is in the east at Chappal Waddi. This mountain is 7,937 feet (2,419 m) tall.

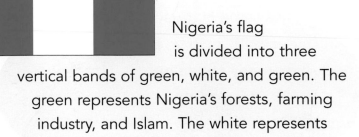

Nigeria's flag is divided into three vertical bands of green, white, and green. The green represents Nigeria's forests, farming industry, and Islam. The white represents peace and unity.

Nigeria's largest river, the Niger, is Africa's third-largest. It is also the river that gave Nigeria its name.

In Nigeria, 50 percent of the people are Muslim, 40 percent are Christian, and 10 percent follow African religions.

Nigeria's money is called the naira. The exchange rate often changes, but 132 nairas equaled one U.S. dollar in 2004.

English became Nigeria's official language during British rule, but it is most Nigerians' second language. At school, Nigerian children learn their ethnic language along with English or French.

As of July 2004, there were 137,253,133 people living in Nigeria.

Nigeria is one of the world's largest producers of oil.

Proud to Be Nigerian

Flora Nwapa (1931–1993)

Flora Nwapa was one of the first internationally published African authors to publish books in English. She wrote novels and short stories about Nigeria's people, places, and problems. Many of Nwapa's stories were about women who shared their experiences of living in Nigeria. Her self-published children's books taught important lessons about being good. In addition to publishing, Nwapa taught at colleges and universities around the world and held positions in civil service. Flora Nwapa died of pneumonia in 1993.

Olusegun Obasanjo (1937–)

Born in Abeokuta in the Ogun State of Nigeria, Obasanjo would become Nigeria's first civilian, or nonmilitary, president. Obasanjo began his life of service to his country after high school. Upon graduation, he joined the Nigerian army and received military training in England, the U.S., and Nigeria. His efforts in Africa's Congo and the civil war in Nigeria made him a war hero.

From 1976 to 1979, Obasanjo was elected Head of State of Nigeria. In 1999, he was elected President of Nigeria. From 1999 to 2002, he tried to solve many of the problems between Nigeria's ethnic and religious groups. In 2003, he won a second term in office. In his reelection speech, he promised that he would work harder to make Nigeria's future bright.

Hakeem Abdul Olajuwon (1963–)

Hakeem Olajuwon is considered one of the world's greatest basketball players. At eighteen, Olajuwon left his home of Lagos, Nigeria to play for the University of Houston. He led his team to three national championships. After college, Olajuwon played for the National Basketball Association's Houston Rockets. In 1993 and 1994, Olajuwon led the Rockets to two NBA titles. He was voted the best NBA defensive player, Best NBA Center, and Most Valuable Player (MVP).

Olajuwon was also a fourteen-time all-star and a five-time all–defensive team player. In 2000, he was traded to the Toronto Raptors. He retired in 2003 with 20,000 points and 12,000 blocked shots and rebounds. At the end of his career, he could only complain that he "didn't thank God enough!"

Find Out More

Books

The Distant Talking Drum: Poems from Nigeria by Issac Olaleye. Wordsong, Honesdale, Pennsylvania, 2001.

Nigeria by Rob Bowden and Roy Maconachie. Raintree, Chicago, Illinois, 2004.

Nigeria by Patrick Daley. Raintree Steck-Vaughn, Austin, Texas, 2002.

Nigeria in Pictures by Janice Hamilton. Lerner Publications, Minneapolis, Minnesota, 2003.

Web Sites*

World Almanac for Kids Online: Nigeria
http://www.worldalmanacforkids.com/explore/nations/nigeria.html

Nigeria: CIA World Factbook
http://www.odci.gov/cia/publications/factbook/geos/ni.html

Videos

Globe Trekker: West Africa. VHS, 555 Productions, 2002.

Lonely Planet: West Africa. VHS, Lonely Planet, 1997.

*All Internet sites were available and accurate when sent to press.

Index

Page numbers for illustrations are in **boldface.**

About the Author

Patricia J. Murphy writes children's storybooks, nonfiction books, early readers, and poetry. She also writes for magazines, corporations, educational publishing companies, and museums.

Patricia lives in Northbrook, Illinois. Through her Nigerian research, she has made new friends from Nigeria. She hopes to travel there someday. In the meantime, she will make akara and play ayo with her nephew, Erik.

Acknowledgments

Special thanks to Dr. Patricia Ogendengbe, librarian of Africana at Northwestern University, Evanston, IL; Professor Felix Obialor, Chicago, IL; the Nigerian Consulate; and the Nigerian Embassy.